THOUGHTS FROM A
"SICK" MIND

Thoughts from a "Sick" Mind

shAmyAble

To order additional copies of this book, contact:
Xlibris
1-888-795-4274
www.Xlibris.com
Orders@Xlibris.com
779250

CONTENTS

THE DEDICATION

This one goes out to all the people
Who followed raunchy fan fictions,
While remaining the class prude.
This one goes out to the girls
Who got into trouble with their teachers,
For punching the boy who was being rude.
This one goes out to all the people
Who said they were too busy to go to the party;
Because the thought of going home,
Blasting your headphones,
And eating ice cream out of the container,
Was so much more appealing.
And this one goes out to the people
Who found their own way of healing.
To all the ones
Who have a hard time expressing themselves.
To those
Who go spelunking into their own mind.
To those
Who imagine other realms.
And those
Who daily leave the world behind,

Who else has spent hours locked away
With themselves and been okay?
I can't be the only one
Who's taken myself on a date.

To my loners
And my stoners.

To my weekly leaf blowers.
To my readers,
To my dreamers
And my midnight cleaners.
To my procrastinators,
My anti-haters,
And to all the "order takers"

Because we are so awesome.

And don't ever let someone
Who has never experienced what it's like
To dance under the stars,
With no more music then the critters in the leaves,
Tell you that what you are doing is weird.

Because GOD DAMNIT WEIRD IS BEAUTIFUL!!

And it's colorful.

And I'm going to let the colors fall
From me
Like the earth is my canvas
To leave a mark on.
I'm not going to worry
About where the colors fall
And god damnit neither should you.
Your colors are so bright!
And if someone is being blinded by you,
Then just hand them a pair of shades,
And tell them it's okay.
Not everyone can handle being weird!

I'm From

I'm from broken homes
And wise beyond years.
From shattered hearts
And unseen tears.
From sibbling bonds,
And making the best of the worst.
From long black veils
And a slow moving hearse,

From happy days
To tragic nights.
From hugging sisters
To brothers fights.
From seeing it all,
And still staying happy.
To being on Celexa
For feeling pretty crappy.

From big bright cities
And small knit towns.
From wanting slow dances
In long lavish gowns.
I'm from turning the worst
Into the best.
And rolling hills
That are way out west.

I'm from sarcastic jokes
And always having fun.
From joking at dinner

And playing in the sun.
From simple times
Playing nintendo DS.
To throwing down cards
And calling BS.

From not having much
And still smiling all day.
From playing outside
On a warm rainy day.
From reading and writing
At an early age.
From sitting in my room
And turning the page.

From country to rap
And rock to blues.
From listening to music
Instead of the news.
From black vinyls
To white 8 track tapes.
From shiny CD's
With interesting shapes.

From being god fearing
And having laugh lines.
To looking back
On all the good times.
It's the little things
That make you who you are.
Every bump
And every scar.

I'm from a funny family
With beautiful eyes.
This is who I am
Without any lies.

ANXIETY

Did you know that…
No I can't say.
For if I say it,
You will do one of two things.
You'll be mad at my redundance.
Or,
You won't like it
Because you didn't already know it.
So I sit here in silence.
And there you sit.
Wrapped up in obliviousness.
No!
I won't suffer.
Im going to tell you!
Here I go!
Get ready!
Get set!
…
No.

YOUNG

Holding back the silent sobs,
Facing your biggest fears.
Telling everyone you're fine
As you wipe away the tears.

Locked away inside your room
Tears falling on their own.
You cannot stop them as they fall.
Loneliness chills to the bone.

Wishing for a sweet escape.
Praying for release.
And knowing that if you do
You'll never be at ease.

Now you feel the suffocation
As loneliness fills your lungs.
You never knew it'd be so hard
To be so god damn young.

A State Of Understanding

WHAT THE FUCK IS WRONG WITH ME?!?!?!?!?!?!?!

Well Amy,
You were diagnosed with PTSD
And don't forget about anxiety.
You've also had depression since about 13
And you've been know to have suicidal tendancies.
What you need to do,
Is get a clue.
The world does not revolve around you.

They want me to
Listen to
Their diagnosis,
And let it control my next move.
But I don't think they get what I've been through.
My doctor,
At 16,
Told me
The reason I can't sleep,
Is because I needed to turn off the TV.
But she didn't see
Me
Wake up in a cold sweat
Every night,
At exactly 3
In the morning.

Trapped in mourning!
What she didn't get
Was that I didn't let
My moms fiance' take me to bed.
Which made sick in the head.
And that's why sometimes
I just wish I was dead.
That doctor didn't understand
That it was wrong to ask about it
Right in front of my dad.
I wish I had
Told her the truth,
But I was so mad.
And those black lies in that moment
Didn't make me bad.
They told me that it wasn't my fault
That it happened,
But it was my fault
That I still let it affect me.
They told me
Like everyone else does
That I just need to toughen up.
Well listen up!
There is nothing wrong with sensitivity
Maybe,
You need
To learn how to be,
Less of an insensitive asshole.
Us broken ones don't need to get stronger.
Ya'll just need to ponder
The thought,
That we all go through shit.
And just because you handle it differently
Doesn't make me sick.
Step off your pedistal
Of fake happiness
For one minute.
And realize we are all in it

Together.
So we should intertwine our emotions
And keep them tethered,
In understanding
Forever.

While The World Sleeps

I sit outside while the worlds asleep.
Smoking a cigarette while they all dream.
I sit here and ponder in self doubt,
And ask myself what life is all about.
I wonder if I can make things right,
And in the darkness I find the light.
Good things can come from an evil place.
Just gotta take things slow,
Not focus on the race.
I mean the race of human kind,
Who all walk around as if they are blind.
There's so much hate and so much greed,
Motivating me to do good deeds.
I can't be part of all the pain,
Despite the fact that it'll always remain.
Cause if just one person can spread the love,
Then who's to say it can't come from above?
Everywhere I go I try to spread the joy.
Not gonna keep to myself and play it coy.
So put your hands up if you're just like me.
And let's spread the love on the count of three!

PINK

Artificial moments,
Created by drunken stupors.
Moments of clarity,
Created by emotional breakdowns.
Moments of thought,
Provided by nonsensical brain jumble.
Thoughts such as:
What's a girl to do?
And, oh shit, I need super glue
And why is sadness represented by the color blue?
Why can't it be pink?
It just makes me think
About what brings people to the brink,
Where they're surrounded by darkness
Without a clue.
And you would describe that
As the color blue?
I wish it was pink.
Cause when you blink,
It flashes before your eyes;
And that phrase makes me think
About people who've died.
People who've tried
To just do well
While they lived in hell.
Okay!
Okay!
I'm off topic.
But there's more reasons too.
About why pink should be sad

And people should stop blaming it on blue.
See pink
Makes you think
About easter,
Or womanhood,
Or about that dress I wore
That night on the bleachers.
About happiness in general,
All because it's so bright.
And I wore that dress with sneakers
Because I was told to.
If I didn't I'd be uncool.
I didn't know about the rule.
Oh you don't know the rule either?
Well where I come from,
I found out too late,
Was that wearing a dress with sneakers
Meant that you wanted to date.
And in this shitty day and age
It also means,
Let's go into the woods
And get in the position to pray.
But I was 15;
Too scared to do it
And permanently labeled
A stupid tease.
You see,
It's not about pink.
It's about accepting that blue
To you,
Is not blue to me.
Just like you smile,
When you think
Pink.

I Rose From The Ashes

The sun was low,
The stakes were high.
I rose from the blood in the enemy's sky.

The sky drew dark.
My blade drew cold,
And I took their mind of pure white gold.

I pierced it deep into their mind.
And shined my sword
With the blood of their kind.

I took their land
And stole their fame.
They should have never invited me to the game.

For I conquered what
The enemy had,
And made their ending so damn sad.

And I cannot cry for their defeat,
Because now my ending is so very sweet.

HOME

The pen hits the paper
And I instantly feel safe.
No more angst.
No more pain.
Just my words
That no one can take away.
The itty bitty ball
On the tip of my favorite tool
Has it's own way of protecting me,
And embracing me.
When I'm not writing
My mind is racing
And I'm chasing
A thought,
That I can never seem to catch up with
But my heart is pounding!
I'm running out of breath.
My lungs want to fall out my chest
And suddenly,
The paper finds it's way to me
And I can breathe again.
No more playing pretend,
I'm finally home.
You see
Home is where your heart is,
And I guess that means
My home,
Is in the thousands of trees
Who have sacrificed their lives
So that I could find peace

In the middle of the night.
When sleep is the dream
And I have nowhere to escape.
So I open to a new blank page.

IMAGINARY CONVERSATIONS

I have a lot of imaginary conversations.
No,
I don't need help.
I just obsessed the details.
Like that one time in Middle School,
When I was practicing breaking up with Rhovin.
It's not you it's me.
No that's stupid.
My mom says I can't be with you.
Ew!
Too,
Romeo and Juliet.
Sorry dude, it ain't working.
Hours spent trying to write a script
For how this moment should go;
And the next day
I got to school,
Sat next to him in class
And I passed him a note.
Because I couldn't plan it any better way.
Dear Rhovin,
You are an amazing boyfriend
But I never see you outside of school.
You get better grades,
And your parents probably want you to go to Harvard.
I'll probably go to some run-down Community College
So we should just go our separate ways.
Signed Amy :)
He shortly passed it back
OKAY

All caps.
OKAY
Okay. Okay. Okay. Okay.
That word playing on repeat
As we went our separate ways.
For one full year we didn't speak.
He was my first kiss.
The first set of lips
That were put on mine by choice.
I was second in that class that year.
He was first.
He was always first
I've imagined lots of conversations with him since then.
I'll ask him how he's doing,
Or if he found someone.
Tattered half-truths will come as a response.
And as I sit in silence,
I treasure those made up conversations.
The fake dialogue
That will never come.
I moved to Arizona the year we didn't talk,
But I always kept in contact in my head.
One day my freshman year,
I spent my lunch period on the phone.
That conversation only had 5 words.
Rhovin killed himself this morning.
Never said goodbye.
Never got to ask why.
I guess he didn't want to go to Harvard.
And now I'm stuck here
Conversing with myself.
Keeping memories of him
Tucked back in my heart,
On the dustiest of shelves.
Because no matter how I fixate on the words,
No matter how I practice the delivery,
I'll always be stuck in the epitome
Of that note.

The last note.
He was the first heart I broke.
He was the first hand I held.
He was the first person I knew
Who died
By suicide.
And with so many of the first that he was for me
He will also always be,
The last person I talk to
Before I go to bed.
Even if he's just in my head.

TWO TYPES OF PEOPLE

Hate!
Oppression!
Bullies!
Pain!
All inevitable.
Get over it.
Don't let it get to you.
Why are you crying?
Don't do that!
Just let it roll off your shoulder.
You'll get used to it!

Love!
Acceptance!
Leaders!
Joy!
All possible.
Grow from it.
Let it build you.
Cry it out if needed.
It's okay!
Collect it and examine it!
It'll leave you alone!

PUBLIC EDUCATION

I walk around this campus with a smile on my face.
While I deeply contemplate the human race.
Why's he such an ass?
And why does she cry?
Why do some of these teenagers just want to die?
Where did we go wrong,
Making them not want to move on?
We talk about progress,
Yet we just push them on.
These kids by the dozens,
Not put into ovens,
But forced into schools
Where we teach them
Only how to follow rules.
No individuality,
No creative flow.
They're asking questions
And being answered with no.
Do your paper this way,
But turn your cheek that way.
Never letting them excercise their brains
At play.
All day
They're forced to sit in a room,
And we expect them to learn that way?
You'll need this in the real world they always say.
Yet these kids are walking around in a scheduled haze.
Not taking in knowledge,
But pushing it away.
Because how is humanities

Going to help my friend who is gay
And getting punched in the face,
Man that shit is some insanity.
We see all these people lost in the vanity.
Yet never teach them about the past
With clowns,
Who tricked crowds
Of the same kids
Who grew up following the rules.
Instead of questioning the ones putting them in schools.
Ya'll wonder why they grow up and lash out,
When they grew up not knowing how to hash out
The problems that they are facing on the daily.
Like who do I want to be,
And what's with the crazies?
Are they really insane,
Or just questioning authority?
Do they really need help,
Or are they ones who are talking
To the hoards of people
Who never spoke out at the lies?
Never grew up asking questions like why?
Why is my life less significant than yours?
And why do I have to choose,
Between one of the doors?
Why am I limited to what you say I am?
And why can't I chose
To just stay who I am?
Instead of one kid,
Who was full of color and art.
He was shunned for bad grades
Being told he ain't smart.
It's to those kids I say:
You should stand up and scream!
That they will never be able
To tell you what it means,
To be a person with questions and doubt.
It's okay to fall down.

And sometimes to pout.
It's okay to feel alone
And out of place.
Take your time son,
This shit ain't a race.
Just stop,
And breathe.
It's alright to be afraid!
Just remember your worth,
Doesn't come from a grade.

The Normal

Let's embrace the normal.
Let's embrace the simple things.
Let's savor the 2 a.m. talks,
About mindless rememberances,
Over burnt cigarette butts
And empty bowls.
Lets not forget the significance of mint chocolate ice cream,
As our lives drift from vibrant and clashing colors,
To harmonious rainbows
That sway in unison
To our hearts beating as one
While we sleep entangled in each other.
Let's sail hand in hand,
Over the threshold
From chaos and adventure,
Into wildly perfect syncopation.
And let's never forget,
That while times may get hard,
No song is finished
Untill at least one note
Dares to venture off into the unknown world
Of the off beat rytham.
You can be the melody
That brings meaning
To my lowley life of harmony alone.
You can be the bell
To fill the void of unseen tears
And haunting silences.
Let's stay friends
Through the late nights,

And wake to the rising sun,
And sleepy good mornings.
Let's jump head on
Into embracing the normal.
And let's never forget the moments
That brought us together,
And set the foundation for forever.
Let's embrace the normal.

BLACK, WHITE, AND GREY

I don't see the world in black and white.
I see it in shades of grey.
And no,
That doesn't mean I want to tie up my ex-boyfriend
And fuck him in the ass with a strap on.
Even though lets face it,
I totally have.
It just means,
That not every question
Has a definitive answer!

My life in Matte Charcoal Grey,
And my best friends is almost white.
With a simple smoke screen,
Glossing over every part
Of her beautiful soul.
And I've met people with souls as black as night.
So to say that there is only one way to be
Is just as ignorant,
As saying that sex
Shouldn't be scary.

I've looked into the eyes of a beautiful man,
And his world is shrouded in battleship grey.
He wakes up everyday,
Ready for the war
That will unfold in his brain.
And the little girl who used to live down the lane?
Well her world was nickle.
Because she had so much growing to do,

That even the slightest insult
Could bend her world in half,

I see the world
For all the shades between black and white.
And it never has a plot twist.
A plot twist is too simple.
Those of us who live in the in-between
Have had our hearts destroyed with a chainsaw,
And our worlds crumbled with an instant look.

But that's the beautiful thing
About black and white,
And grey.
They all coexist
And balance.
And leave us wondering
What beautiful shade
Will walk into our life next.

SEX

Sex is beautiful!
And scary,
And gross.

Sex will hurt.
It will make you feel like your heart
Is falling out of the most private parts of you.

Sex is emotional.
Sex is evil.
Sex is the mover of worlds,
And it has the ability
To change someones opinion.

Sex can teach you lessons.
It can teach you love.
It can teach you patience.
It can teach you to care about someone,
Other than yourself.

But we live in a society
That sexualizes everything!

So you see,
Sex is also the enemy!

I'M SORRY

Poems can be apologies,
And I have so much to be sorry for.

Your breath danced off my skin,
While I thought about what I needed to do tomorrow.
So I'm sorry for not faking it again.

Your fingertips danced up my thigh,
While my heart broke on the inside.
So I'm sorry about the lack of time.

Please hear my rhyme.

You were my light!
You were my crime!
And I lost it all,
Because I was so busy looking for a sign.

I'm sorry that I broke your heart.
And I'm so god damn sorry
That I wasn't honest at the start!

But this is me now!
Not who I was then.
So hear my apology,
And know I would do anything
To have it back again!

Round One

I've got a lot of words
Kick boxing each other
Behind my cerebral cortex.
So please excuse the stress.
And I'm sorry,
If my facial expression
Is an unreadable mess.
I must confess,
It's not always easy
Living in my head.
I hear these voices,
But they don't tell me to kill.
They just push away the will.
They push away the motivation,
And leave me in perpetual hesitation
It's just that aggravation,
The frustration,
It takes over sometimes
And leaves my mind racing.
The voices and words
Get pushed together,
To create a symphony
Of confusing word clutter.
That builds up
And blocks my creative flow.
Dagging my positivity low.
I start to show
My overstressed anxiety.
That dwells inside of me,
And pushes me away from society.

I get too absorbed in me.
Why can't I just step away?
Why can't I find the words to say
What I'm feeling?
Why can't I explain that
Sometimes,
Your eyes pierce.
And sometimes
They burn.
But mostly,
They make my insides melt.
I've never felt
So charged up.
Like walking on felt
Then touching an electricity belt.
My brain is fried,
And I've tried
To scream this out.
So undignified!
Just because I'm tired
Of fighting myself
All the time.
What's wrong with my mind?
I'm done.

ARSENIC

I've always wanted to be with somebody
Who could lift my heart to the moon.
But baby,
You make me want to build a ladder
And walk there myself.

I've always pictured someone
Who could wrap my anxiety in a fire blanket,
And calmly remind it
To stop drop and roll,
After it's been set on fire by my depression.
But you hand me a lighter.

I've always envisioned someones arms on my back
As we stand,
Chest to chest,
In that moment when two hearts beat as one.
And the cinemtogrephers always made me believe,
I would be
With someone who made me feel safe.
And sometimes,
It feels like you are pushing me off a cliff!

But as I free fall
I realize,
There is a trampoline at the bottom.

And when I thought you were pushing,
You were mearly urging me to bounce back.
When you hand me a lighter,

It's to melt the ice around my brain.
Because there is no gain
In wanting someone to save me.
You see that I have two legs to walk on.
And if it feels like you are trying to hand me a gun,
It's because you want me to kill the pain
And doubt.
If you take my map away from me
And tear it to shreads,
It's because you want me to find my own route.
So thank you for supporting me.
And the next time you send a care package
Full of arsenic,
I'll use it to slaughter the voice in my head
That tells me I'm better off dead.
Rather than letting it seep in to the negativity
That engulfs my tearducts,
And feeds into my own insecurities.
This is hard for me!
But you
Keep sending me tools
While you sit back and wait patiently
For me to see
That it's not just about me
And you
Are one of the greatest people in my life.
So tonight,
I thank you.

Let Me Own My Name

I've heard people say,
I'm not part of this system.
But I think that there's something
That everyone's missing.
Our names are for collateral,
Not individuality.
If you write it in all caps
You'll take away all personality.
And leave behind
A monetary stream,
Of what you're "worth"
Or so the government deems.
That corporate mindset
Taking over society.
And I'm standing at the bottom
Screaming: you can't look down on me!
But they can.
Because my mom signed my name away
Before I could even say dad.
It just makes me mad.
And no one's aware
Because they're all too scared.
And this includes me.
Theres so much I can't see,
And so much I don't know
About who runs the show.
Seriously!
Think about it.
Who is actually in charge?
And why?

It's about time
We start opening our eyes.
It's time to try,
To understand the lies
That run our lives.
Before we die.
Just so the law makers
Can bank more,
And take more,
And spend more.
Which feeds back into
The same corportions who,
Are running it all.
As we all,
Fall
Right
Into it.

Meet My Addict

Look in the mirror,
That's your reason not to.

But what I see,
When I look at me,
Is a fuck up addict
Who'll never find peace

See
The addict in me
Is the personality
Who cares so much
About what others think.
But he's also the one
Who'll lend you some gum.
Or let you bum
A cigarette
Or two
Because he knew
The feeling of desperation.
So he gives his all with no perspiration.

See,
My addicts the kind of guy,
Who'll teach you to find
All the answers to life.
Even though he doesn't quite get it himself.
But it's not to be condescending,
Oh no,
It just makes him glow

On the inside to know
That he helped ease someone's troubles.
Because his are doubled
And he is so fucking troubled.
Because there's always rebuttal.
Makes him curled up,
Huddled,
In the fetal position.
Always wishing
For someone to save him,
And he's craving
To not feel so alone.
To feel like there's actually something
Behind the concept of home.
Okay. Okay.
I admit it,
It's a little weird that my addict's a guy.
But that's because I wish
Someone would get,
That I feel lost in this world
Of unhappiness.
I can't do it no more.
I just stare at the floor.
Or the ceiling,
Or the table,
Or the wall,
Or anything
To help me forget it all.

Opposing Worlds

I cannot string the words together,
Exlaining how you make me feel.
I've always been a hot tub
Boiling over 100 degrees,
And you are my giant ice cube.

If you were to fully invest,
You would lose who you are.
Yet my heart has grown so hot,
That I crave the icy touch.

But I don't want to hurt you!

So I keep on boiling.
While you sit in deep freeze.
And we long for no more than eachother,
Yet remain in opposing worlds.

DON'T PATRONIZE ME

My God you are tiny!
Do you even eat?
You need to put some meat on those bones.
You tell me this,
As if,
My stature couldn't be
Genetic.
As if,
There's something wrong with me.
Can't you see?
I'm a fucking person.
Not some child,
Eyes wide,
Searching for the answers to life.
With sheltered perspectives
And ignorant bliss.
That's a lot to carry for a little girl.
Don't lose your smile honey,
It's a mean world.
As if,
I haven't seen
The dark alleyway,
That life hides away.
As if,
The dark corners of life,
Have never engulfed my mind.
As if,
Fears claws,
Have never slowly slithered up my jeans,
And made me scream.

Because how could it?
I mean I only weigh 80 pounds
And I'm under 5 foot 3.
So I must be,
Young
And innocent.
As if,
Being a small person,
Means my heart can't stretch
As vast as an ocean.
As if,
My personality,
That's deeper than the crevices of the Grand Canyon,
Couldn't possibly
Be held together by 80 pounds of depression.
Don't worry you aren't done growing yet.
Well I'm sorry sir,
But I'm pretty sure
I'll never fit your normal size standards.
Don't tell me to grow
Because you don't know
What it's like to have to climb up on cabinets.
Or what it's like
To wear your head taller than the Stratosphere in Vegas.
I'm sorry sir,
But you aren't wrong.
I will keep growing.
But not into the Barbie doll,
You all
So desperately crave.
It's my mind,
It can stretch out into the horizon,
And my attitude will grow
To reach out into the heavens.
Hey short shit!
Hey midget!
Don't throw it to her,
She probably couldn't reach it.

But that's okay.
To them I say:
I'll just go on my way,
And build a super sweet pillowfort.
I would invite you in but
You would probably be too big to fit.

Note To Self

You are not a reject!
You're not the scattered pieces
Of a jigsaw puzzle,
That someone never finished.
And you are not defined
By your mental illness!
Don't let society make you believe
That your heart is just something
Designed to be seized
There's so much more to you
Then your self-inflicted scars,
So don't lock all your good parts
Into neatly labeled jars.
You have wings,
Yet you don't use them to fly.
But I'm here to tell you
That it's okay to try.
It's fine to want to see it all.
And I'm saying it's okay to fall.
But don't be scared to live,
Just because life forbid
A normal childhood.
So as an adult you should
Accept that your only constant
Is you!
And being self-absorbed sometimes
Is what you need to do.
I know it's scary
To do it alone.
But trust me, my friend,
That's when you'll find home.

Letter To My Addict

Today I decided to write a letter to my addict,

Dear addict,
No the world isn't going to end today.
And no, I don't have any spare change.
And just because you whisper sweet nothings
Behind my brain,
Does not mean I'm insane.
Dear addict,
It's all going to be okay.
Because if it's not,
Then that means Mama lied.
And you tried
For no good reason.
Dear addict,
I know you feel anxious,
But that's just me
Trying to take back my body.
Heres an eviction notice!
And according to the statistics you only have 90 days
To leave me alone.
Dear addict,
You need love.
But for what?
So you can feel as if you're someones moon
And stars?
You have scars,
Remember?
And how can you expect someone to love you,
When you can't even look at yourself?

You need help.
Dear addict,
I'm sorry for calling you an asshole.
Even though you're the reason
I had to stay awake until 4 in the morning;
Staring at my fucking ceiling.
Instead of healing,
I had to listen to you
Yammer on.
About how we'll never find our fairytale,
Our one true love,
Our special bond.
Dear addict,
I know you think you're all alone,
But you are wrong.
There are no chains around our split wrists,
Nobody held that gun to our head,
And we have never been left for dead.
Dear addict,
Every time you thought you were done,
I was the one
Who kept going.
Every time you left me alone with my thoughts
And left me to rot,
In whatever shitty situation you got us into that day,
I said it's going to be okay.
That was my strength!
The strength of someone who decided to say:
You can't control my life,
And this is MY God damn body.
Dear me,
You are NOT your addict!

I Am Single

I am single!

I fucking hate those words.
When someone asks me if I'm single,
I say: yes, but I'm not available.

I'm not trying to say
That I'm a strong independent woman,
Who don't need no man.
I'm trying to say that I'm a fragile mess,
Who needs to get her shit together
Before she can unload it on someone else.

My dad asks me if I'm seeing someone
And I say nope!
He asks why not…
Um…
Dad?
Aren't you supposed to want me to stay away
From vag thirsty assholes?
And I get scalded for my language.
See I'm so "single" that I let my father scaled me,
Even though I'm an adult
And live SEVERAL towns away from him.

My friends asks me if I get lonely.

Well no shit.
I sleep in a king size bed by myself.
But let me tell you how fucking great it is

To throw my pillows wherever I want,
And sleep at whatever angle I want,
And eat in bed!
I can let my cat on the bed.
I never have to argue over what to watch.
I never have to pause it for anyone else.
I can rewind the scene if I missed it.
I can binge watch something on my own schedule.
And I can keep the fucking captions on!

To all the ladies out there tonight,
I have only shaved my legs once
In the last two months.

Now I know what you are thinking,
That's fucking gross.
I know it.
But do you know how freeing that is?

I wouldn't say I'm single,
I would say im under personal construction.
I am building my own foundation
And I am starting from the ground up.

I AM SINGLE!

I get wine drunk,
And dance with my cat
Who hates dancing.
I do my own laundry
But I never put it away.
My rooms a little messy,
But that's okay.
I eat take out about
Four times a week
And I sometimes wear the same jeans two days in a row
Because I don't interact with enough people
For anyone to notice,

Any you know what else?
When my roommate isn't home,
I pee with the door open
While talking on the phone with my mom!

Thats right I'm single.
And there is nothing you can do about it.

COVERED IN BLACK

You talk a lot of shit,
About this generation and those to come.
But what you seem to forget,
Is that they're your daughters and sons.
You say discipline is gone,
And respect is just a myth,
Yet your generation stood up
And plead the Fifth.
So maybe it's time
We start sharing responsibility for this shit.
You say technology is killing us,
And we need to get a clue.
Then fail to even mention
That it was invented by you.
You put the whole fucking country
Into crippling debt.
Then created the iPhone,
So what did you expect?
You taught us how to barter,
And taught us not to steal.
Then left us broke and hungry
Thinking about our next meal.
While you're sitting lavishly,
Trying to make your next deal.
As we try to heal,
With what remains we have,
From the aftermath
Of your generations path.
So I ask:
Why are so many documents covered in black?

We didn't storm into Vietnam.
We didn't start a war.
We didn't create classes
To divide the rich and poor.
Y'all did that shit.
So don't sit and tell me,
That there's something wrong with reading poetry.
At least we dream.
Which is more than you can say.
I could rant for days,
About how you treat the gays.
Our generation wants love!
And y'all just want beef.
So you should sit down and listen,
Cause I'm not making this brief.
Let's talk about Saint Louis.
Or maybe Rodney King.
Or can we discuss the drugs you're giving the military?
Watergate was you guys too.
And let's talk about those planes that blew.
Your whole generation was completely corrupt.
Which trickled down
And left ours fucked.
We are picking up the pieces
And doing our best,
But there's decades of mistakes
Pilled onto our chests.
I can't stress,
How much of a mess
Was left behind.
Yet you walk around
Acting like you are blind,
To all of the pain that you caused on mankind.

We want answers not excuses.
Yet you're spitting verbal bruises,
To generation who's trying
Just to not feel useless.

As you keep saying
That we are clueless.
And maybe we are.
But did you ever think,
It's because you pushed us to this brink?
So take another drink,
As our generation raises a glass.
To the fact that we are out,
Just trying to kick ass,
In an attempt
To get this country back,
To the way it was
Before you classified it
And covered it in black!

Look Up

Feeling like an alien,
Always sounded strange.
The other kids didn't want to play.
They didn't like that game
Because mommy said
It's not god's way.

When I'm feeling down
I look up.
But not to a "God"
To the possibility that anything's out there.
I'm not scared.
To me:
Religion is restrictive,
And addictive,
But these people have "had their hearts lifted."
So "all of a sudden" they're gifted.
But everyone has potential,
Inside of their temples.
To reach for something greater,
And to exercise their understanding of the universe,
And the way it works,
And why hearts burst.
You see the key to understanding,
Is being able to think outside of the box.
News flash:
Everyone's lost!
And the problem
Is that everyone is so busy
Looking for a destination,

That they create hesitation
In their brain.
And forget
Just to sit,
And enjoy the way.
Enjoy the journey!
There's so much knowledge to gain.
But what if I die tomorrow?
What if I don't get that job?
What if I'll always be stuck in sorrow?
What if,
The key to everything,
Is to just let go of fear?
Shed as many tears
As you can,
Because your tears are washing away your old mindset
As your brain develops
Into
The new
You.

Printed in the United States
By Bookmasters